CHILDREN WHO DON'T SPEAK OUT

Children who don't speak out

About children being used in child pornography

Carl Göran Svedin
Kristina Back

Rädda Barnen
Swedish Save the Children

Rädda Barnen (Swedish Save the Children) works for children and young people based on the UN Convention on the Rights of the Child. We fight child abuse and exploitation and work for the protection of children in Sweden and all over the world. We provide assistance to these children and amass experience through practical action. We influence public opinion, values and attitudes in society through information and education.

Rädda Barnen's Förlag publishes books for people who work with children in order to disseminate knowledge concerning the situation of children and provide guidance and impulses for new ideas and discussions.

ISBN 91-88726-58-4

© 1996 Rädda Barnen and the authors

Editing: Kristina Holm
English translation: Peter Cracknell
Graphic design: Typ & Grafik
Cover: Helen Miller Crafoord
Cover photo: Berno Hjälmrud, Bildhuset

First edition: 1
Printed by Scandbook, Falun 1996

Foreword

The aim of the Rädda Barnen organisation is based on the United Nation's Convention on The Rights of The Child. This convention forms our vision. We believe a child's basic human rights and needs should always be respected and that children should be protected from exploitation and abuse.

Rädda Barnen is releasing the report "Children Who Don't Speak Out" to focus attention on the issue of child pornography. Every child pornography production documents one or a number of cases of child sexual abuse.

The purpose of this report is to show how children suffer from abuse. The following reference is taken from article 34 of the Convention on The Rights of The Child:

The states subscribing to the convention undertake to protect children from all forms of sexual exploitation and sexual abuse. To this end the states will take all possible measures – national, bilateral, and multi-national – to ensure that:

- no child is able to or is forced to participate in any illegal sexual act
- children are not exploited in prostitution or in any other illegal sexual activity
- children are not abused in pornographic sexual acts or exploited in the production of pornographic material

Lisa Hellström
Rädda Barnen

Contents

Introduction

During the 1970's in USA and the 1980's in Sweden we identified and learned a great deal about the occurrence of sexual abuse and the effect such abuse had on children, how to detect its early signs and how to work to achieve co-operation between the different authorities. It was also well known that pornographic material was widely available in the form of magazines, newspapers and videos. In spite of all these factors there has been little discussion about the damaging effects of pornography on potential perpetrators and the children that are participating in the production of pornographic material. Instead of drawing attention to child pornography journalists have tended to turn a blind eye to publishers of pornography and not analysed the phenomenon. Politicians have also largely distanced themselves from the problem. The whole matter seems to have been swept under the carpet as if it does not exist. Both journalists and politicians refer, in this context, to the "right of free expression".

Definition

By child pornography one means a text or an image – i.e. photo, slide, film, video or computer program – that is intended to evoke a sexual feeling, fantasy, or response in adults. Different countries have different definitions and there are problems defining pornography both as regards content and recipient age.

History

Pornography is, in itself, nothing new and can be traced back to a variety of early art forms from different countries. It was however with the introduction of photography some 150 years ago that it became possible to mass produce and distribute images, including those of a pornographic nature. There is however very little similarity between the so-called "French post-cards" and today's close-up pictures of advanced sexual acts in child- or violent pornography.

Until 1968 it was rare to find children featured in pornographic material (Anson, 1980; Pierce, 1984). To present a more innocent image adult pornography producers started to use adults with a youthful appearance. Gradually a market developed for child pornography and children as young as three or four years old became involved. As this trend developed children could be seen in every conceivable sexual position and act. By the end of the 1970s a much wider market was rapidly being established in the USA and it was estimated that about 300,000–600,000 children under 16 years old were participating in the production of this material. It was also well understood that about 7 percent of all pornography depicted sexual intercourse between adults and children (US Gov, 1977). In Sweden we have seen a similar trend during the 1970s and 1980s largely as a result of the abolition of the law (in 1971) relating to order and morality offences. A range of magazines with names such as *Lolita, Children-love, Boys-intensive, Lolly-pop* and *Schoolgirls* ap-

11

peared on the market and were widely available. At the same time an enormous number of amateurish ciné-camera child pornography films were produced and sold in shops and by postal order. Gradually public opinion reacted against the expanding pornography market and this led, in 1980, to changes in the law forbidding the production and distribution of child pornography material in Sweden. For this reason most pornographic material currently in Sweden was produced before 1980 or originates from abroad, principally from South East Asia.

To estimate the actual amount of Swedish produced child pornography has been difficult as preceding the two Swedish exposed pornography operations, 1992 and 1993, there have not been any seizures of child pornography collections. It is though unlikely that commercially produced child pornography is a large industry in Sweden. The latest technical developments from video techniques to the current CD-video techniques, computer and databases systems make exposure of illegal production even more difficult (Rädda Barnen, 1994).

Legislation

There were few states in the USA that had legislation forbidding the production and distribution of child pornography until 1977, but after that year the majority of states introduced their own legislative control that was subsequently reinforced by federal legislation. According to federal law the possessor of more than three child pornography films may be sentenced to ten years' imprisonment. The legal amendment was passed in 1986/7. In Great Britain the possession of child pornography was made illegal in 1988. Other countries have waited until more recently to make possession illegal – Nor-

12

way (1992), Germany, France and Canada (1993), Austria (1994) and Denmark, Belgium and Estland (1995). In Finland legislation is pending, and is also being considered in many other countries.

Current Swedish legislation concerning child pornography is regulated by the criminal code (CC) as well as two pieces of constitutional legislation – the Freedom of the Press Act and the Freedom of Speech and Expression Act.

The criminal code states that a person who depicts children in pornographic pictures that are intended for distribution or is the distributor of such material will be fined or may be sentenced to a maximum of two years in prison (16 Chapt. § 10a). The law took effect in 1980 but the range of penalties that could be imposed was made more severe in July 1993 as the maximum previous prison term was six months. The period of limitation was also changed from two to five years.

The law does not consider that a strict age limit should be used in defining what is a "child" but considers instead that it is a person still developing his or her sexual maturity.

As production of child pornographic material often presupposes sexual abuse then the full provisions of the Criminal Code Chapter 6 are available (see Table 1). The sections of the law used most often in child pornography cases are *sexual exploitation of minors* (6 Chapt.4 §1: CC):

"If a person has sexual intercourse with someone who is under eighteen years of age and who is his offspring or in his foster care, or under his custody or supervision, then that person may be sentenced for exploitation of a minor and receive a prison sentence of a maximum of four years. Unless stated previously in this chapter the same crime is

13

committed if a person has sexual intercourse with children under fifteen years of age."

Or *sexual molestation*, if the crime is considered to be of a less serious nature (6 Chapt.7 § 1–2: CC):

"A person who, in a case not previously stated in this chapter, sexually touches a child under fifteen years of age or incites a child to participate in an act of a sexual nature may be prosecuted for sexual molestation and be liable to a fine or be sentenced to a maximum of two years imprisonment.

A person who through force, seduction, or some other improper means entices someone who is between fifteen and eighteen years of age to carry out or participate in an act of a sexual nature, may also be prosecuted for sexual molestation if the act is considered to be a part of the depiction of a pornographic image or, in cases where an image is not being produced, to be considered a pornographic pose."

This means that it is not just illegal to distribute child pornography but even to exploit children up to 18 years of age in the production of pornographic material.

The age and relation of a child are not relevant if the crime being considered is rape (Section 6 Chapt. 1 § CC) or forced sex (Section 6 Chapt. 2 § CC). Penalties imposed for sexually related crimes vary from fines to a prison sentence of up to 2 years for sexual molestation and up to 10 years for rape. Limitation periods for the different crimes and the penalty terms are given in Table 2. The limitation period for sexual abuse was altered a few years ago and is currently calculated as 10 years from the day the victim had their fifteenth birthday, for crimes according to Section 6 Chapt. 1–4 and 6§§, and in other cases, 5 years from the same date.

According to the Freedom of the Press Act it is not illegal to obtain or possess printed pornographic material such as books or magazines, and the same applies to material presented in the form of pictures, films, sound-recordings and videos under the Freedom of Speech and Expression Act. When child pornography was criminalised the constitutional law was revised so that is was also a crime to depict children in pornographic material if the intention is to distribute the pictures. Distribution was considered to consist of a greater circulation than just one's closest friends.

One has then, at present, a constitutional right to buy, possess and distribute child pornography material provided that distribution is limited to one's immediate circle of friends.

Previous research

Child pornography use

Criminal investigation has shown that nearly all paedophiles collect child pornography (Lanning & Burgess, 1989). This means that the paedophile's interest goes beyond just looking and focuses on collection. An investigation (Hartman, Burgess & Lanning, 1984) found that there are four types of collector. The first type – *the closet collector* – keeps the collection secret and is not directly involved in child abuse. He purchases his material discreetly. The second type – *the isolated collector* – as well as collecting is also involved in child abuse but keeps his activities secret in the fear of being caught. His collection consists of both his own and purchased pictures. The third type – *the cottage collector* – shares his collection and his sexual activities with others, but does not have an interest in financial profit. The last type – *the commercial collector* – produces, copies, and profits financially through sales and is also engaged in child exploitation.

Lanning and Burgess (1989) consider there to be many reasons why paedophiles collect such material. They say that paedophiles can collect to satisfy, support or strengthen their compulsive, impelling, urgent sexual fantasies about children. Alternatively there may be a need to confirm and legitimise their sexual disposition.

From a criminal perspective one can see many different ways in which child pornography can be used. Child pornography may be used to arouse sexual excitement before subsequent abuse, or as a way of reducing a child's reticence to participate. The pornographic pictures can then be used as a way of blackmailing a child to continue the relationship or to dissuade the child from speaking out. Alternatively pictures and videos may be used as mementos or trophies that may, in turn, be copied or exchanged. Finally there are direct commercial considerations through production, copying and distribution.

What effect does pornography/child pornography have on the consumer of such material?

The connection between pornography and child abuse, particularly sexual abuse, has only been sporadically researched. Most research has focused on the connection between pornography and adult sexual behaviour.

Pornography has previously not been considered to directly encourage violent sexual acts, even if it can indirectly lead to damaging sexual treatment of children (Knudsen, 1988). As late as the 1970s a commission set up by the American president reported that pornography didn't have any damaging social affects (US Gov, 1970; Mason, 1989). This view was supported by certain studies that indicated that sexual crime declined when pornography was more easily available (Kutchinski, 1973). For many years there was a predominant model ("the catharsis model") that suggested that the presence of pornographic material in society could reduce sexually related crime. This understanding gradually changed and an investigation in 1986 by the U.S. General Prosecutor's Commission on Pornography identified a number of areas where pornography could be considered to cause significant damage. The connection was established between pornography, sexual violence and child abuse. The previous model has been progressively replaced by an "imitation model" (Silbert, Pines, 1984).

Pornography has been reported to stimulate rape-related fantasies in rapists (Marshall, 1985; Abel, 1985a) and influence the perpetrators of child sexual crimes (Abel, 1985a) as well as lead to increased interest in divergent sexual activities among 39 percent of offenders (Abel, 1985b). Repeated exposure to pornographic material can influence an individual's understanding of sexuality and the nature of a relationship, increasing acceptance of physical violence and reducing the sympathy felt for victims (Knudsen, 1988).

Consequently there is no reason to believe that there is a distinction between how pornography in general, and child pornography in particular, affects the user. This means that individuals looking at child pornography alter their perception of sexuality, violence and abuse. Information compiled about paedophiles gathered during house searches has shown that they possessed a large amount of sexual material (photographs, magazines and videos) relating to children (West et al, 1978; Schetky,1988). It is however difficult to decide from this type of retrospective investigation the cause and effects. It is difficult to determine whether it is divergent sexual interests that lead to an interest in child pornography or child pornography itself that stimulates the desire for sexual acts with children.

Even if people's reaction when exposed to pornographic material varies enormously it is considered that adolescents are particularly receptive to the influences of pornography (Marshall, 1989). A number of writers have reported that an early and frequent contact with pornographic material can be related to sexually divergent behaviour (Becker, Stein, 1991; Condron, Nutter, 1988; Carter, Prenty, Knight, Vanderveer, Boucher, 1987). The results are not however clear-cut. Condron and Nutter (1988), for example, found no connection between an early exposure to pornography and later sexual crime. In a similar study comparing young sexual abusers, young violent criminals and young non-violent criminals the results showed that the young sexual abusers were reported to have had earlier and increased contact with pornographic material as compared with the other groups (Ford, Linney, 1995). An investigation by Marshall (1988) showed that men who had sexually abused unacquainted adults and children had used pornographic material more often than those committing incest and more often than non-abusers. In addition it was noted that a large percentage of abusers looked at pornography before committing a sexual crime. In yet another study using lie detectors with young sexual offenders a connection was established between exposure to hard-core pornography (in the form of videos) and the number of female victims that were subject to abuse (Emerick & Dutton, 1993).

The same phenomena can be seen from a victim's perspective. Silbert (1989) reported that in one survey, 22 percent of 178 female street prostitutes abused as children said that the abuser used, or referred to, pornographic material in connection with the crimes. Such material is used in different ways. Some perpetrators use it to coerce children into submission, others to legitimise the act so that they see it as acceptable behaviour, and a third group uses pornographic material in self-stimulation preceding sexual abuse. Thirty-eight percent of the prostitutes stated that pornographic pictures had been taken of them when they were children.

What are the consequences of being exploited in child pornography?

Internationally a number of writers have noted the difficulty in defining the limits of what are considered the consequences of pornography, abuse, and prostitution (Baker, 1978; Pierce, 1984) see figure 1. Children that are exploited in child pornography are automatically exposed to abuse, as it is rare that simple naked photographs are taken. The photographs normally depict advanced sexual activities in the form of physical contact, masturbation, adult and child sex, and sex between children. In addition children exploited are found to come from underprivileged homes, lacking in child care (Collings, 1995). This also means that children coming from underprivileged circumstances, for example children running away from home, are vulnerable to becoming economically dependent, selling their bodies for sex and pornography. This group currently forms the core of those children in different countries that become street prostitutes and is the group targeted in the expanding sex-tourism trade. It is therefore a complex web of interactions that is being studied, and it makes it extremely difficult to distinguish between the psychological effects of abuse, exploitation in child pornography and long-term neglect in upbringing by parents. It is essential to use statistical analyses where a number of variables are analysed together (Kendall-Tacket et al 1993).

Child pornography is often associated with so-called "sex rings" (Burgess et al, 1984). Sex rings can be categorised into three different types. One type consists of one adult leader and a number of children and there is no exchange of children or child pornographic material to other adults. The second type is made up of a group of adults forming a well-structured organisation recruiting children, producing pornographic material and arranging exchange/sale of children's sexual pornographic services – a syndicate structure. The third type may be considered to be a transitory structure between the other two. In a study of 62 children who had been exploited in so-called sex rings it was possible, based on a two-year follow-up study, to establish different reaction patterns (Burgess et al, 1984). The four reaction patterns identified were integration of the event, avoidance of the event, repetition of symptoms and identification with the exploiter.

Children categorised as displaying an *integrating pattern* were those that could talk about their experiences without it causing great anxiety. They blamed the perpetrator, concentrated on the future and functioned well at home, among friends and at school.

Those showing an *avoidance pattern* either denied the experiences or refused to actively speak about them as they still gave rise to feelings of anxiety or distaste. These children were still scared of the perpetrator and had a tendency to live for the present without future plans. Stress could bring on the reoccurrence of earlier symptoms, sometimes leading to depression or self-destructive behaviour. Relations in the home and with friends were strained and schoolwork suffered. These children still felt shameful of their participation in the abuse.

Children showing a symptom *repeating pattern* were those found to have developed a chronic post-traumatic stress syndrome. This consists of many symptoms, and such children are severely ill at ease when the events are discussed and they are driven by powerful feelings of blame and shame. They blame themselves and cannot get the earlier events out of their minds. Relationships at school and among friends are poor. They often display oversexed behaviour and there is therefore the risk of continued exploitation.

21

Children that *identify with the exploiter* continue to defend the offender and repeat their own trauma through sexually approaching other children. They also show other antisocial symptoms.

Finally the study showed that children who had been exploited or used in pornography for more than one year had the most serious symptoms. They identified with the exploiter significantly more often than the average exploited child.

In an investigation carried out in Leeds, England over a two-year period there were 31 sex rings exposed in which 334 children (296 girls and 38 boys) were exploited by 47 offenders (Wild, 1989). The sex rings gave rise to 4,6 percent of all police reports relating to sexual abuse and 6,6 percent of all sexual abuse prosecutions over the two-year period. Pornographic photographs had been taken in 13 percent of the rings and in a further 13 percent pornographic material was shown to children. Behavioural problems were common among children who had participated in the rings for longer periods – in particular amongst those that had assumed a leadership role. Other children who were involved with the ring to a lesser extent were not known to the authorities. This was due, for example, to diviant behaviour patterns (Wild, Wynne, 1986).

Internationally, clinics and researchers agree that there are three factors that are decisive in determining how serious a trauma may be expected in a child exposed to sexual abuse. These factors are the nature of the abuse, the length of time that the abuse has occurred, and the perpetrator/child relationship. For children that have been victims of sex rings there are additional factors that can contribute to an increased level of emotional and social trauma (Hunt & Baird, 1990). These factors are, of course, the larger number of perpetrators – increasing the influence on the child's degree of trust in adults, the incidence of serious threats, and documentation via photographs and videos. Hunt considers that documenting events contributes to an increased sense of joint responsibility, disgrace, shame, humiliation, and helplessness. It is also an effective means of dissuading the victim from speaking out.

In a study of 100 juveniles that had participated in child pornography (6 to 21 years old, with an average age of 14 years.) Silbert (1989) charted the victims mental health and reactions at three stages – while subject to exploitation, at the time the exploitation was exposed, and a number of years later.

During *the exploitation period* the children that had participated for shorter periods had symptoms such as vomiting, headaches, loss of appetite and insomnia, and often described themselves as temperamental and experiencing difficulties in socialising with friends. The children suffering exploitation over a longer period spoke of more intense feelings of isolation, anxiety, and fear.

At the time *the exploitation was exposed* (only 1 percent themselves expose the offender) there was a great feeling of conspiracy, and they had little trust in adults. This period was described as traumatic and chaotic.

Years later the children's feelings of disgrace, fear, anxiety and negative self-esteem had been further traumatised by desperation, hopelessness and psychological paralysis.

Such a trauma is set to continue indefinitely in the knowledge that films depicting the individual in degrading circumstances are being spread nationally and internationally. "Who has seen it and do they recognise me?" These feelings can cause a continuing severe state of anxiety after the actual exploitation has ceased (Mulvey and Haugaard,1986)

As regards the treatment of children and adolescents that

are exploited in child pornography the documented material available is very restricted. In an article Schoettle (1980) describes the three phases of an analytically based treatment of a 12-year-old girl. These phases were "ticket of admission", "ambivalent phase" and "integration phase". They are broadly in line with general principles relating to the treatment of children that have been exposed to abuse.

Which children are exploited in child prostitution?

In the USA it is considered that the largest group of children at risk are those who run away from home. It is these adolescents that are so extremely vulnerable to adult exploitation – in prostitution and/or in pornography (Pierce, 1984). It can, together with petty theft, become a means of survival (Dudar, 1977). Others are exploited by their own parents or by other adults in the neighbourhood. Children involved have not then, in general, reached the age of puberty (Lanning & Burgess, 1989).

National background and the background to the investigation

Rädda Barnen have in two previous reports (1991 and 1994) tried to describe and chart child pornography and child prostitution in Sweden. There is no Swedish investigation that has studied the exploitation of children in child pornography or the consequences thereof. We are not aware of any study that has tried to compare information documented in seized material with what children, when questioned, have stated about the degree of their participation.

During the last few years the police have exposed two child pornography operations – the Huddinge operation in 1992 and the Norrköping operation in 1993. In the course of both of the subsequent investigations it was soon established that the bulk of the child pornography was produced in South East Asia with South East Asian children but it was quite likely that Swedish men were the perpetrators. European children seemed to be included in some of the material and it was suspected that some footage was produced in Sweden with Swedish children.

In the Huddinge operation the police received a tip-off in 1992 via Interpol in Germany. A German paedophile had bought child pornography from two Swedish post-office box addresses. The Huddinge police kept the post-office boxes under surveillance and apprehended two men, born 1928 and 1954, who had been selling child pornography by postal order using the post-office box addresses. The two men's houses were searched, revealing at least 160 child pornography video and ciné films. They discovered complete, expensive, and technologically advanced equipment for the production, editing and copying of video films. They also found large numbers of child pornography magazines, newspapers, correspondence, orders, accounts and lists of addresses. One of the men had tried to flush a record of customer purchases down the toilet. In the younger man's oven under some metal trays they found three lists of customer addresses in Sweden, Norway and abroad. In total they found 80 Swedish and 15 foreign addresses. Following analysis of the seized material they could establish that the video films made up a kind of library where customers, according to their sexual preferences, could order particular film sequences that were then spliced together to make a new video film. In addition to commercial sales, films were loaned and exchanged. The younger man had private photo albums with shots of naked or semi-naked boys from his journeys to South East Asia, which confirmed a direct link to sex tourism.

Both Huddinge men were arrested on suspicion of sexual molestation and sexual exploitation respectively, as there was reasonable cause to suspect sexual crimes had been committed in connection with photographing young boys in sexually compromising positions. Both denied the charges and were released after two weeks. In 1993 they were both convicted of pornography distribution. The older man received six-months' imprisonment and the younger man four months in prison. However the younger man was subject to further charges during the investigation period. The investigating police officer Lars Lundin, on further examination of the material evidence, succeeded in identifying part of the wallpaper in the man's flat. In this way three boys were identified and a further three were questioned. The man was subsequently convicted to four years imprisonment for sexual abuse. A man from central Sweden had sent in a video to the post-office boxes under surveillance showing that he himself had sexually exploited a 12-year-old boy. A house search revealed video films, photographs, photo albums containing pornographic pictures and personal photos of young boys. The man was sentenced to two-years' imprisonment in 1992.

In December 1993, one and a half years after the Huddinge operation was exposed and the wider consequences were still under investigation, the National Swedish Police board's post office control unit discovered, in an item of mail from Denmark, a bundle of black and white pornographic pictures. The pictures were addressed to a 25-year-old man in Norrköping who was urged to distribute them further. The man's house was searched and 200 video films and an address register with 15 potential customers was discovered. The man was arrested suspected of distributing child pornography and house arrests were concurrently carried out at 12 other addresses around the country. This resulted in the confiscation of an additional 1 200 films and 13 people were summoned for suspected child pornography offenses. In the Norrköping investigation they continued their attempts, from the films that were considered to be Swedish, to identify victims and offenders. There was a name-plate next to a bathing place in one of the films and this led investigators to a 43-year-old artist in Småland who had exploited two girls. At the time of the abuse the girls were three and 10 years old respectively. The man was sentenced to three-years' imprisonment in 1994, a sentence that was later reduced to 1.5 years by Göta's court of appeal. During an inquiry in Skåne in January 1994 an offender and a girl were identified from a photograph. As a result a 46-year-old man from Stockholm and his 45-year-old former common-law wife were sentenced. The father was convicted of abusing his daughter, son, and his daughter's best friend. The former common-law wife was convicted of having had sexual intercourse with the boy on two occasions. The man was sentenced to in-patient psychiatric care and the woman given a probational sentence and obliged to undergo psychiatric treatment.

In both of these investigations the areas of inquiry were very extensive, involving many individuals and large amounts of confiscated material evidence.

Since the Huddinge operation was exposed there has been very intense debate about child pornography and freedom of speech and of the press. This debate and its various ramifications have been well documented by the journalist Christina Hagner (1995).

The police have so far succeeded in identifying four children associated with the Huddinge operation and five associated with the Norrköping operation. Additional children have been identified, but it has not been possible to establish that abuse has actually taken place. There is also one child, not connected in any way with the two operations described above, that has been identified through a photography dealer.

The police and the child and adolescent clinic at the University Hospital in Linköping have come to an agreement where the police inform the clinic when they have been able to identify children from the material evidence collected, as this gives an opportunity to study how the children have been recruited and what they remember of their involvement. It is a unique situation to compare the children's account with the actual course of events – as depicted by the pictures and video films. Such a study can also give information as to how the children are coping at the present time and how they are fitting into society.

28

Investigation

Purpose

The investigation process has had two main purposes. The first aim was to establish a general profile of the sort of children that are exploited in Swedish-produced child pornography. The questions posed were: What was the child's relationship with the perpetrator? How did they become involved? Why did the participation continue? And last but not least: How did the child feel before the abuse, while it was taking place, at the time the abuse was exposed, and now at the time of the inquiry?

The other main reason was to study how children while being questioned by the police tell about something that we already know has taken place – that is documented in the pictures, the order that the events are related, and how they react and feel when confronted with the questions, factual information, and the pictures themselves. It differs significantly from most police-child questioning regarding sexual abuse, in which the investigator only has access to the information available at the time of the reported sexual abuse.

Other secondary reasons have arisen after the study was initiated and the material examined. These include information on the perpetrator, their paedophile activities and networks. Furthermore the child's role in the legal process is of special interest.

The material

As few children are involved and the cases are of particular interest to the massmedia this account of the investigation will respect the children's and their family's right to anonymity and integrity. For this reason identifying details are not included as it is *child pornography* we want to highlight and not the details of a particular case.

The basis of the investigation has centred on all the children that the police have succeeded in identifying from the confiscated child pornography material in Sweden during the unravelling of the two large child pornography operations. In total five cases or trials are considered. Two cases were associated with the Norrköping operation (four girls and a boy), and two cases arose out of the Huddinge operation (four boys). One girl's case was not associated with the two operations. In both investigations many children were involved but it was not possible to prove that they had been exploited in child pornography and/or sexually abused. In the Norrköping operation three perpetrators were convicted (two men and one woman) and in the Huddinge operation two offenders (both men). In the separate case one male perpetrator was convicted. In total ten children are considered in five separate cases and six perpetrators (five men and one woman).

A summary of the material with details of the children's ages during the time of abuse, when the abuse was exposed and during the investigation is given in Figure 2. One can see that there are large differences between when the abuses started, their duration, and the time elapsing before they were exposed.

Method

We wrote to the five police authorities and law courts with a request to have access to all the material evidence relating to the relevant inquiries and court documents. Permission was granted in all the cases by the police authorities and law courts.

We have carefully scrutinised all the court documents (10 in all) including the pre-investigation protocol, video/sound recorded questioning/interrogation, and seized material evidence. The questioning results have been examined with respect to the children's unprompted remarks, the order in which they relate their experiences, and the nature of the exploitation. This has then been compared to the confiscated material evidence. Strongly expressed emotions and memories arising in the course of questioning have been noted. We have also observed how the children had been recruited and kept involved and whether bribes or threats had been made.

The children and families involved were contacted by telephone and informed about the investigation, and its purpose and form.

Of the eight children that were questioned in earlier investigations five were interviewed in semi-structured interviews focusing on background, upbringing, the account of abuse, experiences both in connection with and after exposure of the abuse, and feelings relating to the stigma of pornography. Other questions related to the help that the children had received in rehabilitation, their current perception of their experiences and their present relationship with the perpetrator.

Seven children completed the self-assessment Youth Self Report that is a self-assessment version of the Child Behaviour Check List for adolescents 11–18 years of age (Achenbach, 1991a).

The report consists of 112 questions and measures the possible occurrence and level of psychic disorder symptoms and behavioural problems in adolescents. The questions are coded 0, 1 or 2 – in which 0 describes the absence of a symptom/behaviour while 1 and 2 describe the frequency of the symptom/behaviour. The method is well tested and widely used internationally in different investigations but is undergoing trial in Sweden and only provisional normative data is available (Gustafsson,1995).

Seven parents (sex mothers and a foster father) were interviewed in a semi-structured manner concerning the child's and family's background, the parents' experiences at the time of exposure, the police questioning procedure, and how the children felt before, during, and after exposure/police questioning. The extent of active social networks, how the child copes socially at school and among friends were all covered along with details of any help that has been sought or received. Finally the parents were questioned about any remaining sufferings, specific problems, and feelings of stigma and how family life has been affected.

The seven parents also answered the CBCL, a report that was formulated by Achenbach and Edelbrock and covers children four to 16 years of age. The report consists of 113 questions measuring, in the same way as the YSR, the presence or absence of a symptom/behaviour in the child. The questions are answered with 0, 1 or 2, as above, and the points are added together to form both a total and different, specific factor points – for example, for internalising and externalising. The higher the total the more severe the difficulties of the child. The point systems of the YSR and the CBCL are not directly comparable. The YSR gives a generally higher point total. The report's questions have been translated into Swedish but the method's psychometric qualities have not yet been conclusively established. At present the CBCL is being reviewed based on data tests obtained from clinical and normal subjects. There is though preliminary data available obtained from Swedish adolescents (Larsson, 1994). The American version is currently the most widely used symptom/behaviour report for scientific use. Accounts of information about standards, reliability, and validity are available (Achenbach, 1991b). In a comparable study between American and Dutch children there was a correlation between the two countries' scales that varied between 0,80 and 0,98, in respect of seven different empirical syndromes (Achenbach et al 1987).

We have also asked to have access to any relevant child and adolescence psychiatric journals or other treatment publications. The investigation is approved by the Research Ethics Committee at University Hospital in Linköping (Dnr. 95232).

Results

Results obtained in the investigation will in general be presented as a whole as the information obtained from a given question is collected from the different sources. Some of the material is presented at the individual level from individual details. The information is group presented when there are obvious group divisions. In one group (seven children – five girls and two boys), now called group A, the children had been exploited by a family member or someone close to the family. In the other group (three children – all boys), called group B, the children had been exploited by a male stranger who had sought to befriend the children. The man was practically unknown to the children's parents.

Family background

The children in group A seemed to come from fairly average family backgrounds. Six of the exploited children lived in normal family units with their natural parents during most of the time that the abuse took place. One child had separated parents and two children's parents separated at a late stage during the abuse period. The 12 parents were all pursuing careers at the time of the abuse although one received early pension due to ill health and another became unemployed during the follow-up period. The parents worked, for example, as an engineer, assistant nurse, in a self-employed business, teacher, computer technician, secretary, receptionist and as a carpenter. Information in the report revealed however that there were periods when parental supervision and energy were lacking – due to divorce, death and work demands, and that they were somewhat credulous in not realising that abuse was taking place.

The children in group B all came from problem families. None of them lived with both of their natural parents. All of them lived under difficult socio-economic circumstances. One family received temporary disability pension and drug/alcohol abuse had resulted in one death. The child was placed in a foster home. Another mother received early retirement (sickness) pension. In all the families there was a lack of child care and supervision.

Relationship to the offender

The perpetrator in the cases of two of the children in group A was the father. The mother was unaware of what was taking place for many years. For one child the abuser was the best friend's father. In the other cases in group A the abuser may be said to show "cuckoo in a nest" behaviour. Trusted and respected by the other adults and liked by the children, no one suspected abuse. The children were naturally drawn to the perpetrator who gave them attention, was aware of their interests, and did things that they enjoyed. Like a young cuckoo he excluded the parents, and the parents appreciated the lightening of their parental workload. The abuser acted, for example, as playmate, babysitter, sports leader, and fishing partner. The perpetrator edged his way into family life and was considered for a long period to be a pivotal figure and often the most important adult to the child.

The perpetrator in group B made contact with the children away from the home, for example, at a flea market or in a square. He befriended the children and then invited them home to play computer games. Further visits followed with more computer games, and the children could loan video films, and enjoy chocolate and sandwiches.

How did the offender initiate and maintain the contact?

The natural father started abusing his children when they were still young. The daughter was still using nappies and her foremost memory at a later stage is that her father said it was normal and that he told her what she should do. He presented the whole process as normal, encouraging her by promising amusing activities afterwards. It was also to be their secret and simple toys were sometimes used as bribes. Another argument was not to make Daddy unhappy. The children trusted their father until they were old enough to realise through the mass media that this was not a normal way of relating. There was an understanding between the children and their father that the children would not tell anyone. The son was told by his father that "people do this to each other because they like each other and because it is enjoyable". Asked why he agreed to participate the son answered "well, he was my father". When questioned, the son talked about his fear of not doing what his father wanted. The father motivated his son to have sexual intercourse with his common-law wife by saying that he "needed a sexual debut with an experienced woman", that is, a form of sexual inauguration.

One girl stated that it started more as a kind of game with friends. The other children describe how the offender first became a "really good friend" long before the abuse started. They were able to talk to the perpetrator and enjoyed different activities together. Sometimes the offender even helped

36

with everyday chores such as homework. Sometimes the contact had been established for a whole year before the abuse started. Thus the perpetrator continued to be an emotionally important adult for the child and through establishing the norms described above and through sexual inauguration, encouraged and stimulated the child's own sex drive. The abuser has also with threats ranging from weak to pronounced and through presents and financial bribes persuaded the children to continue the contact.

The children have made it clear that they felt shame for the things they have participated in, and this disgrace also contributed to maintaining a contact with the abuser. These children had actively sought a contact with an adult and invested energy establishing an emotionally meaningful relationship. It was not that easy to just break it off and see that they had been exploited and deceived by this adult figure.

The period of abuse

The period of abuse is based on the information obtained from the application for a summons, or from the child's and offender's statements if they are in joint agreement.

The total period of exploitation for the 10 children collectively is just over 28 years (28 years and three months), varying from one occasion to over eight years (eight years and four months). Fifty-one years had passed from the first abuse to exposure. Disregarding the two children that are taken to have been asleep during the abuse the remaining children had kept the abuse secret for over 42 years (42 years and nine months).

Consequently we can conclude that none of the children had freely told of the events.

37

Sexual acts of abuse

In respect to the various offences, the crimes accounted for here are those of abuse, not pornographic crimes that are investigated by the Chancellor of Justice.

What actually takes place in the pornographic activities? What have the children been participating in? All the children have been photographed with normal cameras, CD cameras or video cameras. Two of the offenders had also placed concealed cameras in their bathrooms. This documentation has in all cases but one been distributed in varying degrees between different like-minded individuals/customers, in the country and most probably abroad. The acts that were hidden behind the crime headlines and that were nearly always documented in photographs/film were:

- A boy who has been abused in the form of masturbation, oral sex, anal sex, and photographing thereof. (Sexual intercourse with a child).
- A boy has masturbated for the offender, had intercrural sex (between the legs), attempted anal sex, oral sex, and sex with other children (grievous sexual exploitation of children). There has also been two occasions of sexual intercourse with a woman that were video filmed (sexual intercourse with a child).
- A boy has been forced to participate in sexual activities in the form of mutual masturbation, oral sex (forced sex) and anal sex in an intoxicated state with the offender (sexual exploitation), posing and oral sex with a friend (sexual molestation).
- Another boy has been forced to have oral sex with the perpetrator and his own friend (forced sex and sexual intercourse). He was also exploited by being required to pose

and masturbate with a friend (sexual molestation).

- A boy has been persuaded to, primarily, pose naked (sexual molestation).
- A girl has been photographed and exploited in oral sex, sex with a friend and photographed with pens entered into her vagina (sexual intercourse).
- A girl has been subject to posing with various objects positioned between her vaginal lips and in her anus, and participated in oral sex (grievous sexual exploitation of a minor).
- A girl has, over many years, on numerous occasions been abused in intercrural sex, oral sex, being photographed with the perpetrator in different positions, with pens in her private parts, and sex with other children and posing in sexy underwear (grievous sexual exploitation of a minor).
- Two girls have been photographed in their sleep with the offender masturbating above them, stroking their sexual organs and putting a dummy soaked with sperm in one of the girl's mouths (sexual exploitation of a minor). These two children have not participated in the investigation since they by concordant observers were judged to know nothing about the abuse.

Children's reactions at the time of abuse exposure

The reactions vary from relief that it has now been made known, to extremely strong denial and desperation when faced with the need to confront what had happened. One boy described, willingly, the relief of exposure and consoled his mother with "now it's over". A girl describes how she had decided to speak out when she became an adult and moved away from home. Now when she, completely unprepared, saw the pictures of her serious abuse, it felt extreme-

39

ly difficult. One girl considered it a relief that it had all been revealed, but at the same time it was apparent, when questioned, that her attitude showed that she was "proud" and assumed the responsibility herself, thereby protecting the offender.

It is difficult for children to let go of the defences they have used over many years. With unexpected exposure defences such as rejection, denial or isolation no longer work and a flow of confused feelings become apparent. A number of the children were deeply sickened when they saw the pictures, expressing feelings of shame and feelings of having been deceived by the perpetrator. One boy displayed great anxiety and denial during most of the introductory questioning. He didn't want to accept that it was he that appeared in the pictures presented to him. Three of the children also showed a great fear of the offender at the time of exposure.

Reactions among parents at the time of exposure

None of the parents had the least suspicion that their children had been abused and exploited in child pornography. The parents said that at first they didn't want to believe that it was true. It was a considerable shock. They didn't want to believe that it was their child that had been abused or that the adult perpetrator, whom they had trusted could assault their child. They were deeply shaken and describe the initial feelings as disbelief, chaos and panic. This was followed by feelings of anger and a desire for revenge (the father) – mixed with feelings of pity for the perpetrator's tragic fate (the mother). The more long-term problems have been worry that the children have been hurt and feelings of shame that they, the parents, didn't understand what was going on. The mental strain was accentuated considerably due to all the attention from the mass media. There was an overwhelming sense, for the parents and children, that everyone would know who they were and what had happened. Most of the parents considered going underground and moving from their homes. Many difficulties remain, including feelings of embarrassment and an unwillingness to speak, in the family, about the abuse. In the majority of the families there are still close relatives that are unaware of what happened.

Police questioning – the children

Introduction
When the children are questioned they are between 12 and 18 years of age. The number of questioning sessions with the children varies from one to three. Different documenting routines are used. Three of the children are questioned using a tape recorder and five using both sound and video recordings.

At the start of the questioning procedure two of the children are aware of why they are there and six of the children have only superficial knowledge that it relates, in some way, to photographs in which they appear.

What do the children say?
Anna was informed that the police had seized photographs of a sexual nature and that the perpetrator was detained.

Anna who was abused over many years in different sexual acts while being filmed and photographed, says unprompted: "My first memory is when we took a bath together and I was to suck his penis". Anna doesn't remember and doesn't speak, unprompted, about any further abuse. Then she sees the photographs and films and can identify the individuals involved and state how old she was when the abuse took place. Anna repeats many times that she doesn't remember the events and says "I know that a lot happened, but everything is so vague. I cannot be sure of exactly what happened".

Anna doesn't either remember any feelings from the time of abuse. She reacts strongly to some of the pictures and they make her feel sick. When she was about 11 or 12 years old and heard through the mass media about sexual abuse Anna started to get pictures in her mind of the abuse she suffered when she was very young. The images were not complete, but they were images of sexual abuse. (The offender has admitted that the abuse started when Anna was still a toddler).

Björn is told that the perpetrator has been detained because of suspected sexual abuse.

Björn says, unprompted, that the offender wanted Björn to "suck him off". He also states during which period the abuse occurred. He also remembers that he had been together with other children and that they had stroked each other.

Björn doesn't say anything more spontaneously and when he sees the photographs where a woman is having sex with him, he doesn't remember the occasion. He reacts strongly and after a while remembers that it happened on yet another occasion. Björn doesn't remember that he has had sex with other children, but he remembers it when he sees the pictures later. He then also recalls the details surrounding the events.

Cecilia is informed before the questioning sessions that there are video films and photographs that show that she has been sexually exploited.

When questioned Cecilia starts to tell, unprompted, that she remembers playing theatre together with a friend, and that they undressed to put on other clothes. Cecilia doesn't say anything more spontaneously. She has, however, a vague recollection that she has been with other children and that they have examined each other's bodies. She cannot remember an adult being present or that she was photographed or filmed. When Cecilia is shown a picture of how a man subjects her to oral sex, she says with surprise. "Oh! Was this so long ago?" and comments on her own hairstyle. She doesn't seem to be aware of the actual event depicted. Cecilia then feels very ill at ease when she sees the pictures and says that she has now, of course, seen the evidence, even though she cannot remember the events.

David is questioned the same day that he is picked up at the suspected perpetrator's home and taken to the police station. The suspected offender is detained at the same time and they arrive at the police station in separate cars.

David tells how he met the perpetrator and what types of sexual abuse he was subjected to. He tells nearly all of the story unprompted and then answers the interviewer's questions in detail. When it becomes apparent that David met the offender so often and over such a long period, the questioner asks him why he did so. David answers: "I've been so bored".

Erika doesn't know what the questioning session is all about. The questioner starts to tell her that he knows that she has been at the perpetrator's home and that some pictures were taken there.

Erika says that she usually ringed him and was then collected and photographed and that they were nude pictures. She is then asked many questions but she won't say what sexual activities she was subjected to. The events that are outlined by the questioner have taken place in the six months preceding the police questioning. The last event had taken place only a few weeks previously. Erika doesn't say anything about how the suspect has touched her, but it is instead left to the questioner to describe what the offender has said and Erika then confirms that the abuse has taken place. Until then she maintains that she doesn't remember.

Fredrik doesn't know why he is asked to come to the police station. He feels it must be because of his former drug/alcohol abuse.

When he is asked if he has been photographed in the past he replies: "Yes, by the school photographer". Asked for a third time he accepts that he has been photographed "home with a friend". Fredrik doesn't say anything, unprompted, about the sexual abuse he underwent, but restricts himself to talking about what happened in particular photographs he is shown. When the questioner asks if Fredrik had been with the suspected perpetrator on other occasions Fredrik answers: "No – well yes – one time, when I returned some films". Fredrik tells how he rang the doorbell, returned the films and then ran down the steps. When the questioner asks whether anything else had happened he tells of the perpetrator's suggestion that he and some friends should receive payment for particular favours and that they had declined. Then he changed his mind, remembering how they were paid by the offender to masturbate.

Gustav doesn't know why he is to be questioned. When he is presented a photograph showing his face he denies that it is him. He agrees afterwards that he is featured in the photograph and even says who had taken the picture. Then Gustav says that he had been home to the suspected perpetrator but denies four times that he had been there together with friends. After that Gustav doesn't say anything more unprompted. When asked whether he was photographed naked he answers no. When the questioner shows him such a photograph Gustav repeats a further 24 times that "it cannot be me". It is very difficult for Gustav to accept the documented evidence. He becomes extremely anxious, low-spirited and cries so the session is interrupted. In the break Gustav has an opportunity to be with his mother and a social worker. When the questioning session continues Gustav starts to relate hesitantly and disjointedly – how together with a friend, he was threatened into subjecting to different sexual activities, and how they were filmed. Gustav refers to one occasion, but when he realises from the photographs that there had been other occasions he answers "I believe it must have happened a number of times".

Gustav finds it difficult to speak and says after a while: "I just cannot speak about this, I am unable to sleep at nights anymore".

Hans has been questioned by the police before – about six months ago – concerning the suspected man. When Hans is asked if he knows the man in question he replies: "Yes, even though I have forgotten about him. He was in fact a pleasant sort of guy." Abuses are not documented in photos and nor does Hans speak of any while being questioned.

In summary there is only one boy who tells unprompted about sexual abuses; that is David. This is most probably due in part to the short period of time that has elapsed between the abuse and his questioning. David is also the child who shows most relief that the abuse has been exposed. It is he who says to his recently informed mother "now it's over" while at the police station being questioned. The children speak in detail only about those events about which the questioner is already aware, either through the photographs or the suspect offender's account. There is only one boy who

45

speaks about an event that is not documented among the films and photographs seized by the police. He does this in another questioning session two months later. The event described was later confirmed by a legal affidavit. When the boy was asked why he hadn't told about this event at the earlier session he replied: "No, it all comes back once you get sorted out. I remember more and more".

The children's accounts are fragmented and demonstrate the great difficulty they have in talking about their previous contacts with the suspected perpetrator. The children often say that they do not remember. If this means that they have no memory of the event, or if it suggests that it is just to difficult to put into words, we don't know. It becomes obvious however that the events and acts that the child least "wants to remember" are those that are most unpleasant or most offensive. It is these events that probably give rise to the most shame and guilt.

It is apparent that the greater the number of questioning sessions that the children participate in, the more they are able to relate. It is as though they must "digest the memories" before they can relate the events. The sessions are rather like an onion that is peeled; layer after layer is tentatively pulled away.

Police interrogation – offenders

The six perpetrators have been questioned on two, three or four occasions.

The first offender confesses in the first interrogation that at the children's request he had photographed them, but denies distribution of pornographic material stating: "someone must have stolen it". He denies that he had given the instruction but is refuted by the material evidence. In interro-

46

gation number three he admits to sending the film. He also confesses to the abuse (oral, intercrural sex) that he is presented with but emphasises that the child participated voluntarily.

The second perpetrator (a woman) is shown a video film and confesses to having had sex with a boy on two occasions. The woman says that her fellow offender and the boy took the initiative. In the second interrogation the perpetrator no longer remembers the second act of intercourse and claims innocence due to a blackout resulting from a medicine and alcohol overdose. She did not mention this in the first interrogation. It is, however, an extenuating circumstance in the legal judgement.

Perpetrator number three is brought for questioning together with the plaintiff. The interrogation takes place only three days after the latest abuse. The offender admits to having sex with and filming the plaintiff during a 12-month period. He even confesses to having exchanged photographs and films with others. In the second interrogation he tries to minimise his roll and describes the plaintiff as equally forward as himself. In the third interrogation he shows regret and wishes to cooperate. He writes down 13 names of boys he has had contacts with. The offender sees that he has done wrong and feels a certain relief that it has all come out into the open.

The fourth perpetrator is informed that he is suspected of having had sexual intercourse with children and of sexual molestation. He refuses to be questioned without his lawyer. In the next interrogation he denies using force but accepts that sexual intercourse legally occurred. He then doesn't remember where he met the boys, who suggested taking the pictures, or the reason for the photographs. In those photographs where he was himself participating he says that it was at the children's request, putting the blame on the victims. He only admits to the photographed sexual acts.

The fifth perpetrator is shown photographs that a photography shop forwarded to the police. The perpetrator admits that they are his work. He confesses to sexual exploitation of a minor but states that it all took place with the girl's consent.

Perpetrator number six is questioned and admits that he has touched children but denies that he has touched their sexual organs. When he is shown a video film he admits to the acts depicted: "You know, of course, what is on the tape".

To sum up, these interrogations can also be likened to peeling an onion, but the onion has become slippery. None of the offenders give an account of events unprompted, but make statements only when presented with the material evidence. Without exception, they all remember very little and play down their role in the abuse: "It was the children who wanted it". "The boys asked me to photograph it". "I haven't done anything they didn't want me to".

The perpetrators admit to those events that are captured on film or photographed, but nothing else. None of them initially take responsibility for what they have done and say that it was the children who took the initiative. When it is clear on the film that they have given instructions they acknowledge this. Nor do they take the blame for having hurt the children. One of the perpetrators argued that as the children are happy in the photographs then they must have taken the initiative. During an interview with a boy it was just this instruction that he so well remembered. The offender said all the time: "Big smiles, don't forget. You must look happy".

Who are the perpetrators?

A common factor for all the male offenders was that they could be described as friendly, pleasant and interested in children. They found it easy to make contacts with children, socialise with children, and the children liked them. A number of the offenders were involved in club activities for juveniles, for example, scouts and sports (three of them). Four of them may be described as, and admit to being, established paedophiles. Another perpetrator should not perhaps be characterised as established but rather at the beginning of a paedophilic development.

Considering the collected child pornography material a classification may be made, according to Hartman and a colleague (1984). One perpetrator can be described as an "isolated collector", three as "cottage collectors" and one as a "commercial collector" (see p. 16). All of them are interested in photography and knowledgeable too. The majority of the offenders have intermittently, through the years, had mental problems. Four of the five men and the women offender were required, as a result of these acts and others, to undergo examinations conducted by a forensic psychiatrist. Two have had earlier alcohol/drugs abuse problems. Only one had been sentenced in the past for child sexual abuse crimes.

The children's psychosocial health

Time preceding abuse

We do not have any detailed knowledge of how the children felt and functioned before the period of abuse. One child in group A had various behavioural problems while a child from group B had a problem with school truancy. Another child had been having crying fits, getting into conflicts with other children and had become oversexed, but not to such an extent as to cause the school to refer the matter further. In the case of this child it has been difficult to establish the time scale of the abuse.

Abuse phase

All children in group A, except one girl, were described by their parents as fairly problem free during the abuse phase. None of the children showed symptoms that could have been interpreted as a sign of abuse. The girl with problems had various symptoms, both before and after the period of abuse. The problems were accentuated at the time of exposure. One mother can remember that her son was more withdrawn before the time of exposure. Another boy was described by his mother as reserved and unhappy. The staff at school noticed that he went around in a trance and was mentally detached. His sleep at night was also very disturbed. The mother of one of the girls said that the only thing she could remember was that her daughter had problems looking after her personal hygiene.

The children in group B, on the other hand, collectively conform to a clear pattern. They all show obvious symptoms and experience behavioural problems during the abuse period. This is described in two child psychiatric inquiries and a report and is also confirmed by teachers and school psychologists. As regards the parents it varied as to whether they were aware that the child had been having difficulties. During the period of abuse two of the boys greatly increased their school truancy. One boy had problems with butane gas abuse and the school said that all of them had evident problems. Symptoms that were noted were restlessness, depression, hunger, exhaustion, concentration difficulties, aggressiveness, bullying, a tendency to always be out roaming, and sexually advanced behaviour in the form of interest, gestures and language. On one occasion one boy came to school with a whole bag full of condoms. All the boys lacked home support.

Period between abuse and exposure
A grandmother to one of the group A children observed that the girl, who as between 10 to 12 years old, wasn't at all well (the abuse ceased at 11 years of age). The girl then felt unwell during all of her senior-level secondary schooling. She was depressed, suffered from insomnia, and sometimes thought of committing suicide. The girl had herself asked her mother to make her an appointment to see a child psychiatrist. This was just a few days before the abuse was exposed. A group B boy was, at his own request, placed in a foster home during the period between the abuse phase and exposure. His foster home placement was due to his own alcohol/drug abuse, and the boy also realised that his mother was unable to take care for him.

Exposure phase
Exposure, that resulted from the police contacting the children, was a shock for both the parents and the children. All mention a period of increased mental strain irrespective of how they felt previously. The children had hoped that their parents would never hear of what happened. All the children

51

were overcome with feelings of shame and being to blame, as well as developing a real anger aimed at the offender. As a result of all the activity that followed; contacts with the social services, child and adolescent psychiatry or crime victim support services, and Rädda Barnen, as well as the legal proceedings, the subsequent period was very chaotic. All the children suffered. This demonstrates the importance of an effective and well-managed support system for children at such a time. The children were not critical of the police questioner but found the need to remember and talk about the shameful exploitation difficult to cope with.

One girl was critical that she was called for questioning and had to talk about what was for her extremely difficult experiences and then be required to travel home unaccompanied by public transport, just when her whole world seemed to be falling apart. The girl was also annoyed that she could not decide herself when it should all come to light. She had thought that it should wait until she left home and had some independence.

Another girl said that she felt faint while being questioned as it was such an awful experience. For the three boys in group B the exposure phase was associated with considerable mental strain. One boy went to the school nurse and asked if there was something wrong with him. "I feel so confused and chaotic". Another of these boys suffered nightmares, screaming in his sleep and lived in fear of the perpetrator and that he would seek revenge. All three boys were scared of what might happen to them when the offender had served his sentence and returned to the same neighbourhood. One of the boys declared in the interviews that despite his fear of the perpetrator it was "a great relief to talk about it in the police questioning sessions".

Period following
After the trials were over life slowly started to return to something approaching normality for the children in group A. A number of the children took a break from school as every aspect of the exposure phase had disturbed their studies. With the support of their parents and friends, recreational activities, and therapy as required, the children have recovered surprisingly well. One child remains in the exposure phase and is in a crisis with many signs of mental instability.

In group B the problems continue. One child has been moved from the foster home to a treatment institution. The other two still find it very difficult to function mentally.

At the time of investigation
The children were asked, at the time of the interview, to complete a self-assessment report detailing their mental health as they perceive it (the YSR). The parents completed another form (the CBCL report) focusing on their children's psychosocial health (see table 3). We have data on all of the children except one but we do know that this child is still mentally unstable.

The tables show us that the children in group A are mentally more stable than those in group B and that there is a tendency for the boys to have more outwardly discernible symptoms than the girls, and this is no surprise. The most common difficulties that the children themselves reported are, in order: argues a lot (7/7), daydreaming (6/7), a hot temper (6/7), swearing (6/7), thinks about sex (5/7), would rather be alone (5/7), shyness (5/7), brags (5/7) concerned with neat and clean and concentration difficulties (5/7). Two of the boys reported that they found it difficult to stop thinking about their girlfriends. The problems that the parents were most aware of in their children were: a wish to be alone (5/7), argues a lot (4/6), stubbornness (4/6), concentration difficulties (3/6), disobedience at home (3/6), poor school-work (3/6), secretive, keeps things to self (3/6), sulks a lot (3/6) and temper tantrums or hot temper (3/6).

The children's sexuality

The children have been exposed to sexual abuse during a period of their lives when they are themselves undergoing sexual development and starting to discover their own bodies, how they function, and to form their own sexual identity. The touching of their sexual organs leads to a progressively increasing association with pleasure and heightened desire. It is principally in the initial stages of the contact with the perpetrator that it is likely that the children's desires/sexuality are stimulated. This is apparent too when studying some of the confiscated photographs and video films. Some of the children have also, in police questioning and the interviews, described a curiosity and desire to actively participate, especially early in the relationship. These children have not had the possibility to develop these sexual feelings at the pace and in the manner appropriate to their age. It is natural for children before puberty to share their growing curiosity and experiences with their contemporaries. In place of this they are required to share their first sexual feelings with an adult, sometimes of the same sex, in a relationship that isn't equal or mutual. The relationship has been dominated by a display of power and directed by the adult need for sexual gratification.

Sexuality is normally an area that is guarded by a sense of integrity and that most people consider to be very private. In these cases the children have also been exploited to expose themselves and their sexual feelings on film or in photographs with the risk that an unknown number of people will gain access to them. Is it not clear and inescapable that the children's sexual development is effected irrespective of which traumas they have experienced. A number of the boys in the investigation said in the interviews that they had questioned their sexual identities and nearly all had wondered how it would work out in their relationships with a boy/girlfriend later in life. Some of them also described "flashbacks" that they have experienced when they are together with their boy/girlfriends. In addition the children completing the report forms often mentioned their obsession with sexual thoughts (5/7). This contrasts with the parents declarations where in no case had they noticed the symptoms that one might associate with sexual problems or oversexualized behaviour. In all probability it has been something that they have felt unable to talk about or accept.

Adjusting to normal life and social support received

Anna said that through all of her senior-level secondary schooling she was depressed and had thought about committing suicide. She was 11 years old when she realised, through the massmedia, that the experiences her father had subjected her to were criminal acts. She decided to protect her mother and decide herself when it was the right time to expose the abuse. It was when Anna met her boyfriend that she sometimes got "flashbacks" of the events. She gets on well with her friends and enjoys various recreational activities and other interests. Anna has felt both hate and sympathy for the offender, if it is the case that he repeated an abusive act that he himself was subjected to.

Anna left school, worked in a fast-food restaurant for a

year and then continued studying at a local adult education institution. She is not scared of being recognised from the photographs and films as she was only small when the events took place. Anna does feel though that it is unpleasant that other men, by looking at her, can persuade other children that it is a normal act. Anna tells us in the interview that she was well received by the crime victim support services. After that she went to Rädda Barnen's Boys' Clinic eight times to discuss her problems. It was Anna that broke off the contact. Anna tells us that she has had a difficult time from the period of abuse until the present day. She does feel though that she is gradually getting better. At the time of the investigation Anna seems symptom free, according to her own self-assessment report and her mother's judgement. Now Anna can speak in a well-informed way about her experiences and even express views in the mass media debate on the subject. She thinks that it is important that other abused children can tell someone of their experiences. The most important thing is that children are informed early, for example, through child care agencies and school, that these are abnormal acts. This gives the conditions necessary to be able to speak out. Referring to Burgess's and colleague's classification Anna is judged to have integrated the experiences (see p. 21).

Björn also had fairly close contacts with the crime victim support services and he had two sporadic conversations at the Rädda Barnen's Boys' Clinic counselling sessions. He chooses not to, even today, talk very much about his experiences. He has never been academic, and changed school after the abuse was exposed. Björn is now studying motor mechanics at sixth form college and is extremely involved in motorcross sport in his free time. His mother considers that he now has only mild symptoms/difficulties, whereas he would say that he is problem free. Referring to Burgess's and colleague's classification Björn belongs to the group with an avoidance behavioural pattern.

Cecilia went on one occasion to the child and adolescent psychiatric clinic to talk through her experiences but didn't pursue the contact after that. Her mother says that she is now symptom free, functions well and is studying on a post-sixth form college nursing course. Cecilia also considers herself problem free, according to the TSR. At one stage she tried to help a friend who had also been sexually abused. Referring to Burgess's and colleague's classification Cecilia is judged to have integrated the experiences.

David had one-on-one therapy for nearly one-and-a-half years; twice a week at first and then once a week. At the same time his parents had 22 consultations and David participated in about half of them. When these finished after about two years David was mentally fairly stable. At the time of the investigation his mother considers him to be problem free. He himself feels that he does have some difficulties but only those that he would consider fairly normal. David is also very involved in motorcross and is taking his driving licence. He broke off his sixth form college studies as he was fed up with school and has his own study plans where he will combine studies with working in his father's company. He gets on well with friends. In the past he was scared that he may be homosexual but is now clearly heterosexual and thinks a lot about girls. Referring to Burgess's and colleague's classification David is judged to have integrated the experiences.

Erika was interviewed when the abuse was exposed. There were plans that she should see a child and adolescent psychiatrist and she later began consultations. She had thought of speaking out but was scared that her mother would be angry. Erika is pleased that it is finally all over and doesn't as yet have any aggressive feelings against the perpetrator. She sleeps in her mother's bed and is scared of nightmares. In the past she has been frightened that someone would find out. Now she is scared that she will not know who will see the photographs and films. Erika refuses to spend a night at a friend's house in case she speaks in her sleep and gives herself away. She has previously shown various symptoms and behavioural difficulties that are now accentuated. Both she and her mother consider then that, at the time of the investigation, she is showing quite a number of symptoms and behavioural difficulties. Erika is in the middle of an exposure crisis and is therefore not classified referring to the Burgess's and colleague's model.

Fredrik currently lives in a treatment home. He speaks about "flashbacks"; images that appear when, for example, he is together with his girlfriend. Fredrik has found it difficult to adjust to school, has difficulties with friends, has got into fights, and abused alcohol/drugs on occasions. There are definitely many underlying reasons why Fredrik is not very stable. In connection with the abuse exposure he has had a number of conversations at the child and adolescent psychiatric clinic. Fredrik still describes his fear of the perpetrator and fear of those that might have seen the pictures. He is disillusioned and aggressive both as regards his background and with the offender. He says that when interviewed it is "incredibly difficult" to talk about it. "I just want to forget". Referring to Burgess's and colleague's classification Fredrik has a symptom-repeating pattern with an element of anti-social development.

Gustav is considered in a statement issued by juvenile psychiatric clinic one year after the abuse period to be deeply traumatised and very unstable. He feels worried, anxious, and has nightmares where he screams out. He is frightened of reprisals when the offender is released and is ashamed to talk about the abuse events. Gustav has been recommended to have long-term therapy but this has not been initiated as he has chosen not to attend. At present he refuses to be interviewed and when his mother agrees to participate he forbids her to do so. His mother says that he still finds that it makes him feel very unwell to talk about the events. Referring to Burgess's and colleague's classification Gustav is judged to belong to the category with a symptom-repeating behaviour pattern.

Hans did not have any therapy at the time of abuse exposure and has not had any since. He is at senior-level secondary school and enjoys it there. School has become like his second home. His teachers describe him as very keen to establish contacts with adults. He has plans for the future and wants to be a cook. At the moment he is doing some temporary work at a petrol station. Asked how he feels now (symptoms, thoughts and feelings) he answers: "I have stopped going up to male strangers". He is still scared of being recognised as someone who has appeared in pornography pictures. Of the three boys Hans has had the longest and closest contact with the offender, but at the same time information established in police questioning would suggest that he was also the least abused. Hans is ashamed of what happened and thinks that it is difficult to talk about it, but is still eager to speak out in the interview. In the self-assessment report he described many symptoms and behavioural difficulties. His school said that he didn't feel well after the interview. Referring to Burgess's and colleague's classification Hans is judged to belong to the category with a symptom-repeating behavioural pattern.

To sum up, it has been recommended that all the children would benefit from therapy. Two of the children had a fairly close contact with the crime victim support services after the abuse was exposed. Most of the children, i.e. except one, have not continued with the therapy sessions. In group A one child went to eight sessions, one child to two sessions and one child to one session, while one boy and his parents went to regular therapy sessions for just over a year. One of the children has only recently began therapy. In group B only one child has had a few sporadic therapy sessions despite all the children being recommended for child and adolescent psychiatric examination.

All the children have feelings of shame, fear and anxiety.

Children can develop feelings of shame when their own sexuality is stimulated before they are mentally mature in that way. They have been tempted into forbidden acts, they have trusted a person and become emotionally involved and have then been deceived. None of the children have met the offender after the abuse has been exposed. All of the children maintain that they never want to meet him again. This also applies to those children where the perpetrator was their natural father.

There is only one child of those interviewed who says that he is currently still scared and suffers due to the risk of being recognised as someone who has participated in pornography films. One child reflects discerningly that she is sad about her participation, as it may stimulate other children to submit to such acts.

Significance of a support system and functioning networks

The results of the investigation make it clear that those children that are currently the most stable – that is those who have integrated the events or else through an evasive behaviour pattern still function well – come from group A. These children have also had a satisfactory social network too fall back on after the abuse exposures. Their families have been supportive and in the interviews say that following the initial crisis the family has been brought closer together. The children have also maintained successful relationships with friends and enjoyed a range of recreational activities. The group has established significantly closer contacts with the network of support professions; the therapy aid offered by the social support services, the crime victim support service, Rädda Barnen and child and adolescent psychiatric clinic services. This is in contrast to the group B children. They are all considered to function poorly and display symptomising attitudes and behaviour. These children have not had effective support networks through the family, among friends or through regular recreational activities. Nor have they chosen, or been persuaded, to contact the various therapy support agencies.

Punishments and damages

Following the crimes one male offender was sentenced to confined psychiatric care and a female perpetrator was given a probational sentence and required to undergo therapy. The others received shorter or longer prison sentences (see Table 4).

Damages awarded to the children varied from SEK 27,000 (US $3,900) to SEK 265,000 (US $37,800). One child was

61

not awarded damages as their claim was submitted to the crime victim assessment board too late (within two years of sentencing).

The child in the legal process

In evaluating the basis for the court judgements there was no social inquiry as to the children's upbringing and home circumstances. In only two cases was there a child psychiatric examination report that could highlight the child's emotional state and any mental problems during upbringing, and both before and after the abuse period. Somatic examinations – pediatric or medico-legal – were available for five of the children.

Only two of the children received help automatically from the various social support agencies to come to terms with their situation. The other families/children were not offered and did not themselves seek such contact. In the investigation about another twenty children are named. Some are present in the pictures seized from the perpetrator but not as plaintiffs in the trial. In the preliminary investigation relating to these cases there were only four questioning sessions with suspected victims that were submitted. It is unclear how many other children and parents were questioned.

Summary and discussion

This investigation focuses on the ten children that are the plaintiffs and the six offenders that have been convicted of sexual abuse. Exposure in the various cases has arisen by identifying the children from the seized child pornography pictures. The investigation is unique in that in all cases there is documented evidence of how the children have been exploited. This has created very different conditions for the nature of the questioning sessions with the children and interrogation of offenders than is normally the case in child sexual abuse cases. It has also given an opportunity to study how children, when questioned, feel able to talk about the nature of their exploitation.

We want to stress that although the investigated material and data is unique it is also restricted in quantity, which means that the results must be interpreted with caution.

The first thing that becomes evident is that not a single child has told anyone unprompted of the abuse. During all the abuse years all the children have kept quiet about the events and kept it secret for many years thereafter. There were no spontaneous revelations. The children have kept it to themselves, not telling their parents, friends, brothers or sisters, relatives or other adults. They have not even talked about the experiences with the friend who was with them at the time of abuse. The abuse isn't exposed until the police identify the children through photographs, films and videos. This gives, in the debate that has began in the last few years,

63

a very contrasting picture to the idea that children may invent or present false accusations. In reality the investigation greatly supports the view that children keep quiet and cope the best they can. The so called "child sexual abuse accommodation syndrome" that Summit describes (1983) would seem, from this study, to be an accurate analysis. The investigation also agrees with other studies of child pornography which report that the exploited child doesn't inform others or report to the authorities (Silbert, 1989). The children are filled with shame when they talk about their experiences and there is a great sense of degradation and blame and fear of the possible consequences of exposure.

The second thing that becomes clear in the investigation is that the children do not want to remember and sometimes mentally exclude their earlier experiences. Only when questioned and then shown the pictures and video films can they accept what has happened. This acceptance is usually accompanied by feelings of intense unease. Such a child experiences severe anxiety and has difficulty identifying with their image on the picture. The children relate mainly what they believe the questioner already knows. They acknowledge the most innocent activities first but are extremely reticent to talk about those acts that are associated with the strongest feelings of shame, unease or disgust.

The third thing that we want to point out is the significance of a network of support both privately and professionally. This was identified in a recent Swedish study as a decisive factor in determining the long-term consequences for victims of abuse (Glingvall-Priftakis, Sundell, 1995).

It is our experience that little account is taken of children in the legal process. The attention is focused on the offender. It is the crime that is examined in the law court and with that the perpetrator. The victim – the children – are courteously received but not properly asked as to how they are coping, either in the questioning sessions or the trial. The premise for the judgements doesn't include social inquiries about the children's upbringing and home circumstances. Few children are thoroughly investigated and few statements are available when deciding on the level of damages. In only two cases are child and adolescent psychiatric examinations available that can highlight the emotional state and any mental problems during upbringing – both before and after the abuse. This is in contrast to the well-structured and in our view well-formulated forensic psychiatric examinations carried out on the offender.

The question of damages should also be approached in a different way than is currently the case. It should be clear that an automatic system of control is required between the court and the Criminal Damages Commission as regards reports on damages considerations. That a minor should need to trust an adult (a parent or primarily, a lawyer) to look after their interests is, in our opinion, difficult to understand. In this way a child can lose out on an appropriate compensation.

The police inquiries also show that there are at least 16 additional names of men who have had some sort of contact with the perpetrator as regards child pornography. In addition there are a further 20 names of children, besides the plaintiffs. Some of the children have been questioned but the prosecutors have already obtained sufficient material evidence to establish that there is a charge and the investigation is not being pursued. It is unfortunate when the first occasion that a victim seeks or is offered help is when abuse is exposed through an investigation. It is clear that the primary duty of the police is to fight crime. In these particular cases of abuse, however, a broader police investigation would be a contribution to society's broader interests: that is, to trace all juveniles and adults that need help irrespective of whether this results in a change in the sentence handed down to the offender. It is perhaps the case that in this group of about 20 children there are some that have been sexually abused. There are notes on such material evidence such as "is photographed but with clothes on", "has often been at the perpetrator's during the last year", "naked photographs" etc. It is not just the children's health that may be disregarded but also their possibility to seek and be awarded damages. Since we know that children, primarily boys, who have been abused may repeat their own trauma and themselves become abusers, every possible means to help them speak out is an important measure in protecting society.

We do, however, want to emphasise the police's co-operative and positive attitude to the investigation and to furthering research in this area. The subject is very complex and requires education, direction, and strategic thinking, both as regards children and their behaviour while being questioned, and of course paedophile characteristics.

In one of the cases, concerning two children, they were subjected to the abuse which was video filmed, while asleep. The investigators determined that the children, who were 7 and 13 years old at the time that the abuse was exposed, were unaware of the event and therefore declined to question them. This meant that the investigators indirectly judged that nothing more took place. This may indeed be correct but the decision not to pursue the matter seems strange given that children are regularly questioned when there are much vaguer suspicions of abuse.

Half the children are boys. There are more boys than one would expect given that these are sexual abuse cases. In general one judges that 15–25 percent of children suffering sexual abuse are boys (National Swedish Board of Health and Welfare, 1993). This higher proportion is however consistent with other reports on child pornography and sex rings (Burgess et al, 1981). The police investigations and examinations into these cases have not at any stage pointed to the existence of sex rings.

One of the offenders is a woman. We think that it is remarkable how lightly the legal process has dealt with her and that she is not liable to pay damages to the plaintiff. We do not, at present, know of any case where a man has been shown to have had sexual intercourse with a girl and is not sent to prison; even when he claims to have been under the influence of alcohol. It would seem that the unfamiliarity with female offenders made the prosecutors and the courts more cautious and hesitant. We see the same pattern in other cases where there are female perpetrators.

Finally one can say that it is very clear that child pornography presumes a crime – that of sexual abuse. As it is a crime to produce and distribute child pornography there is good reason to assert that possession of that production may also be considered a criminal act. At present it is a crime to possess/purchase narcotics, stolen goods, and counterfeit money etc. Those of us who have worked with this investigation hold the view that the possession of child pornography is, as regards appropriate punishment, at least as serious a crime as receiving stolen goods. This alternative approach is not in any way an attempt to limit freedom of speech and expression.

We also think that there should be an age limit or a psychological maturity limit determining the age at which a juvenile may participate in pornography and not, as at present, allow a child's appearance – that is, secondary sexual characteristics – to be the overriding factor. As it stands now it is the offender that is most considered. He doesn't need to ask a child's age before that child participates in child pornography.

To briefly summarise our impression of what the investigation achieves – based on a lot of information about a small number of children – we want to include the following points:

- the investigation greatly supports the judgement that children do not speak out about abuse – they keep quiet.

- the investigation emphasises the understanding that modern pornography always presupposes a sexual crime.

- the investigation suggests that there are many more factors than just the abuse itself that are significant in determining how a child will cope with life afterwards and that it is important to further studies in this area.

- the investigation as a whole, and in particular the photographic/film material, poses the question of how sexual abuse and child pornography interfere with a child's normal sexual development. This is an area requiring urgent further research.

Our gratitude

We would like to express our gratitude to all the participating children and families that have confided in us their deepest personal experiences, enriching the investigation and greatly contributing to its completion. They have increased our knowledge and understanding of the nature of abuse and child pornography.

We would also like to thank all the staff within both the police and the law courts that have been so extremely helpful in supplying material information. In particular we would like to mention Lars Lundin and Anders Sundenius. Their involvement and patient methodical work has been instrumental in charting the different pornography operations, exposure of the perpetrators and of the exploited children.

Bibliography

Abel, G.G. (1985). Use of pornography and erotica by sex offenders. Paper presented to the United States Attorney General's Commission on Pornography, Houston, Tx.

Achenbach TM. (1991a). Manual for the Youth Self-Report and 1991 Profile. Burlington, Vermont: University of Vermont, Department of Psychiatry.

Achenbach TM. (1991b). Manual for the Child Behavior Checklist/4–18 and 1991 Profile. Burlington, Vermont: University of Vermont, Department of Psychiatry.

Achenbach TM, Verhulst FC, Baron GD, Althaus M. (1987). A comparison of syndromes derived from the Child Behavior Checklist for american and dutch boys aged 6–11 and 12–16. J. Child Psychol. Psychiat; 28:437–53.

Anson, R. (1980). The last porn show. In: The Sexual Victimology of Youth, L Schultz (Ed.). Charles Thomas Springfield, Illenois.

Attorney General's Commission on Pornography: Final report. (1986). Washington, DC, Goverment Printing Office.

Baker, C. (1978). Preying on playgrounds: The sexploition of children in pornography and prostitution. Pepperdine Law Review, 5, 809–849.

Burgess, A. W., Groth, A.N., & McCausland, M.P. (1981). Child sex initiation rings. American Journal of Ortopsychiatry, 51, 110–119.

Burgess, A.W., Hartman, C.R., McCausland, M.S., & Powers, P. (1984). Response Patterns in Children and Adolescents Exploited Through Sex Rings and Pornography. American Journal of Psychiatry, 141:5, 656–662.

Colling, S.J. (1995). The long-term effects of contact and non-contact forms of child sexual abuse in a sample of university men. Child Abuse and Neglect, 19, 1–6.

70

Commission on Obscenity and Pornography. (1970) The Report of the Commission on Obscenity and Pornography. Washington, DC, Goverment Printing Office.

Condron, M.K., Nutter, D.E. (1988). A Preliminary Examination of the Pornography Experience of Sex Offenders, Paraphiliacs, Sexual Dysfunction Patients, and Controls Based On Meese Commission Recommendations. Journal of Sex & Marital Therapy, 14, 285–299.

Emerick, R.L., & Dutton, W.A. (1993). The effect of polygraphy on the self report of adolescent sex offenders: implications for risk assessment. Annals of Sex Research, 6, 83–103.

Ford, M.E., & Lenney, J.A. (1995). Comparative Analysis of Juvenile Sexual Offenders, Violent Nonsexual Offenders, and Status Offenders. Journal of Interpersonal Violence, 10, 56–70.

Gustafsson P.A. Preliminära data angående YSR. Personligt meddelande, 1995.

Hagner, C. (1995). Rätten att kränka ett barn. Om barnpornografi och yttrandefrihet. Ordfronts Förlag, Stockholm.

Hartman, C.R., Burgess, A.W., & Lanning, K.V. (1984). Typologi of collectors. In A.W. Burgess (Ed.). Child pornography and sex rings. Lexington, MA: D.C. Heath.

House Hearing Before the Subcommittee on Crime (1977). House of Representatives, Serial #12, 95th Congress, 1st session). U.S. Government Printing Office, Washington, DC.

Kendall-Tacket, K.A., Williams, L.M., Finkelhor, D. (1993). Impact of sexual abuse on children: A review and synthesis of recent emperical studies. Psychological Bullentin, 1, 164–180.

Knudsen, D.D. (1988). Child sexual abuse and pornography: Is there a relationship? Journal of Family Violence, 3(4), 253–267.

Kutchinski, B. (1973). The effect of easy availability of pornography on the incidence of sex crimes: The Danish Empire. The Journal of Social Issues, xxix (3),163–181.

Lanning, K.V., & Burgess, A.W. (1989). Child Pornography and Sex Rings. In Zillman D and Bryant (eds), Pornography: Research Advances and Police Considerations. Hillside, NJ: Lawrence Erlbaum Press, 1989.

Larsson, B., Svedin, C.G., Ivarsson, T. Förälderskattning av beteende och emotionella problem hos barn i normal och klinisk population. Föredrag Läkarsällskapets Riksstämma, Älvsjö, 1994.

Marshall, W.L. (1988). The Use of Sexually Explicit Stimuli by Rapist, Child Molesters, and Nonoffenders. The Journal of Sex Research, 25, 267–288.

Marshall, W.L. (1989). Pornography and Sex Offenders. In Zillman D and Bryant (eds), Pornography: Research Advances and Police Considerations. Hillside, NJ: Lawrence Erlbaum Press, 1989.

Mason, J.O. (1989). The harm of Pornography. Adress to the Religious Alliance Against Pornography, October 26.

Mulvey, E.P., & Haugaard, J.J. (1986). Report of the Surgeon General's Workshop upon Pornography and Public Health. Washington DC: Public Health Service.

Pierce, R.L. (1984). Child Pornography: A hidden Dimension of Child Abuse. Child Abuse & Neglect, 8, 483–493.

Rädda Barnen. (1991). En undersökning kring barnpornografi och barnprostitution i Sverige.

Rädda Barnen. (1994). Barnpornografi. En rapport om barnpornografi i Sverige och dess spridning med hjälp av datorer.

Schetky, D.H. (1988). Child Pornography and Prostitution. In Schetky, D.H., & Green, A.H. (eds), Child Sexual Abuse: A handbook for Health Care and Legal Professionals. New York: Brunner/Mazel.

Schoettle, U.C., (1980). Treatment of the Child Pornography Patient. American Journal of Psychiatry, 137;9: 1109– 1110.

Socialstyrelsen (1993). Sexuella övergrepp mot barn. Allmänna råd från socialstyrelsen 1991:3.

Silbert, M.H. (1989). The Effects on Juvenils of Being Used for Pornography and Prostitution. Child Pornography and Sex Rings. In Zillman D and Bryant (eds), Pornography: Research Advances and Police Considerations. Hillside, NJ: Lawrence Erlbaum Press, 1989.

Silbert, M.H., Pines, A.M. (1984). Pornography and Sexual Abuse of Women. Sex Roles, 10, 857–869.

Summit, R.C. (1983). The child sexual abuse accommodation syndrome. Child Abuse & Neglect, 7, 177–193.

Wild, N., Wynne, J.M. (1986). Child sex rings. Brittish Medical Journal, 293, 183–185.

Wild, N.J. (1989). Prevalence of Child Sex Rings. Pediatric, 83, 553–558.

West, D.J., Roy, C., & Nichols, F.L. (1978). Understanding Sexual Attacks. London: Heineman.

Tables and figures

Table 1. Legal penalties of sex-related crimes. 960101

Crime Classification	*Penalty*
1 §	
Rape	2:0 – 6:0 years
Aggravated rape	4:0 – 10:0 years
2§	
Forced Sex	– 2:0 years
Grievous forced sex	0:6 – 4:0 years
3§	
Sexual exploitation	– 2:0 years
Grievous sexual exploitation	0:6 – 6:0 years
4§	
Sexual exploitation of minor	– 4:0 years
Grievous sexual exploitation of minor	2:0 – 8:0 years
6§	
Incest: parent-child	– 2:0 years
Incest: between children	– 1:0 years
7§	
Sexual molestation	fines – 2:0 years
8§–9§	
Procuring sexual intercourse	– 4:0 years
Grievous procuration of sexual intercourse	2:0 – 6:0 years
CC 35 Chapt. 10a§	
Child pornography (distribution)	fines – 2:0 years

Table 2. Limitation periods. 960101

Limitation period, re.CC 35 Chapt. 1§	Maximum sentence
2 yrs.	≤ 1 year
5	> 1 ≤ 2 years
10	> 2 ≤ 8 years
15	for a given period > 8 yrs
25	Life

4§
Crimes re. 6 Chapt. 1–4 and 6§§, and against children under 15 years old, the limitation period is calculated from the day of the plaintiff's 15th birthday.

Table 3. Children's mental health at the time of investigation

Children no.	Points CBCL Total	Internal	External	YSR Total	Internal	External
Group A						
No 1 girl	13	5	2	22	11	5
No 2 boy	24	4	10	22	1	9
No 3 girl	7	1	2	3	0	2
No 4 boy	11	4	4	47	9	19
No 5 girl	60	18	23	89	30	22
Group B						
No 6 boy	43	14	20	71	21	30
No 7 boy	–	–	–	–	–	–
No 8 boy	–	–	–	82	28	27
Swedish averages*						
boys	15 (15)**	4 (4)	6 (6)	43 (24)	8 (7)	15 (8)
girls	15 (15)	4 (4)	5 (5)	45 (22)	11 (8)	13 (7)

*CBCL B. Larsson, 1994
 YSR P. Gustafsson, 1995
** (standard deviation)

Table 4. Legal penalties and damages

Child	Penelty, perpetrator	Damages, children Awarded°/ claimed*	Damages for pain and suffering	Damages for violation of human rights	Damages for permanent injuries
1.		275.000°	50.000	175.000	40.000
2. }	LRV	265.000°	50.000	175.000	40.000
3.		165.000°	15.000	150.000	–

Probational sentence and
in-patient psychiatric care

4.	2:0 years	(damages set at SEK 55,000 (US $7,800) but not awarded due to late application)			
5.	2:0	(awarded SEK 100,000 (US $14,300), but appeal has been lodged)			

6.		90.000*	17.000	70.000	–
7. }	4:0	150.000*	17.000	70.000	–
8.		27.000*	17.000	10.000	–

9.					
10. }	1:6 years	(no damages requested)			

Figure 1. Cause or consequence?